Ralph H. Waggoner

How to Destroy Insects on House-Plants, Flowers, etc.,

In the Window, the Garden, the House

Ralph H. Waggoner

How to Destroy Insects on House-Plants, Flowers, etc.,
In the Window, the Garden, the House

ISBN/EAN: 9783337069629

Printed in Europe, USA, Canada, Australia, Japan

Cover: Foto ©Lupo / pixelio.de

More available books at **www.hansebooks.com**

HOW

TO

DESTROY INSECTS

ON

House-Plants, Flowers, Etc.

IN

The Window,
      The Garden,
           The House.

NEW YORK:
RALPH H. WAGGONER, PUBLISHER.
1892.

INTRODUCTION.

WHAT AILS MY PLANTS? is a question asked more than any other by lovers of flowers and window-gardening; while bugs, beetles, insects, worms, etc., run over their flowers and plants, and appear and reappear so often that the cultivator keeps asking all the year round: "How shall I kill these pests?"

To answer thousands of these questions and help every one out of their difficulties, this little handbook has been prepared, giving directions, *short*, *sharp*, and *decisive*, how to overcome *every insect enemy* that infests flowers and plants out-doors and

INTRODUCTION.

in-doors, which troubles window-gardens or plants; which eats up the vegetables of the garden, which devours the fruit-trees and shrubs and vines, and lives in the homes of anxious, tired housekeepers.

And so it is presented to you, reader, as the result of many thousand experiments and years of experience, of many cultivators, and in every particular its directions have been made simple and practical.

PART I.

Insects in the Window Garden.

RED SPIDER.

Water Remedy.

Look on the outside of the leaves of your plants carefully whenever they seem troubled or diseased, and underneath will be seen from one to an innumerable number of insects, red spiders, which suck the juices entirely out of the leaves of the plants upon which they are allowed to remain.

They increase very fast in a hot, dry atmosphere.

Moisture is sure death to red spider.

The simplest and cheapest possible remedy is *clear water*, forcibly applied to the foliage, more particularly on the under sides, as often as necessary.

Syringe the plants freely in the morning before the sun shines upon them, and in the evening after the sun has gone off them.

Red Spider on Fuchsias—Various Remedies.

Fill a barrel nearly full of water, slake in it about a quarter of a peck of lime, and let it stand until perfectly clear. Hold the plants in the water (bottom up) for about five or ten minutes, then wash them with pure water.

Take two ounces of soft soap to one gallon of water heated to about 140 degrees; dip the plants infested into it for half a minute; let them stand until dry, then dip again in the mixture at a temperature of about 120 degrees for a minute.

A little flour of sulphur dusted over and under the leaves is also efficacious.

The red spider delights in the heat, and the dryer it is the more it flourishes, and consequently the more the plants suffer; and their appearance is attributable to having been kept in a place too dry and warm.

Separate those that are infected from those not touched; do so at once you discover them. They will always be found on the under side of the leaves.

The plants should be taken from the window to a place where water can be used freely. Lay each on its side in the sink, and pour water over and over upon it, and keep doing so as long as any red spiders can be seen. Doing this once or twice a week thereafter will be a good preventive of their return.

HOW TO DESTROY INSECTS. 7

Carbolic Soap-suds.

Some cultivators have succeeded in ridding their window-plants entirely, without removal, by frequently syringing the afflicted plants with carbolic soap-suds.

Hot and Cold Water—Turkish Bath.

"I did succeed with the Turkish bath (as I called it) in exterminating the pest and saving my plant; but I have come to this conclusion, that it is only with Gen. Jackson's "eternal vigilance" that any louse, mealy bug, aphis, spider, scale, or slug can be persuaded to leave after it once gains a strong foothold. The bath was administered in this way: When the thermometer was several degrees below freezing, I took the plant (a large scarlet salvia) to the doorstep, laid the pot on its side carefully, so the soil would not fall out, then took my sprinkler, full of water, so hot I could not bear my hand in it, sprinkled it all over the plant; then used cold water to sprinkle it; then set it in a dark cellar twenty-four hours. This I repeated every few days, and the object was gained. VIOLET."

THRIPS.

THIS is a very dangerous insect, and not easily discerned. Is of a blackish color, with rings of a dirty white color. They are found upon the under side of the leaves, from which they extract their juice. The female, after laying her egg, dies, and becomes covered with a white woolly substance as a protection to her eggs.

Tobacco-smoke, if dense enough, will destroy thrips, but they take more of it than the common green fly.

With only a few plants the trouble is to administer it thick and long enough. In the greenhouse there is no trouble, as the house is filled and the smoke left until it finally disappears.

It probably will be more convenient to give them a sprinkling or syringing with tobacco-water, made by putting a few stems or other tobacco into scalding hot water (enough of the former to make the liquid a light brown), then add soap enough to make a strong suds. This will, if administered as directed, finish the pests in quick order.

THE APHIS, OR GREEN FLY,

Is larger and more easily seen than the red spider. A good, simple remedy, sufficient for purposes of most window-gardeners, is as follows:

Take some tobacco, put it in some water, and let it soak until it looks like strong tea. The proportions may be about one-fourth of a pound of tobacco to three or four quarts of water. This may be applied with a syringe. A brush or a sponge may be dipped into the tobacco-water and used to brush them off. Small plants can be plunged into it, the top downward.

Doctor the sick plant with sunshine, charcoal, and good drainage.

The aphis usually attacks those plants in some way diseased, and when this is the case the plants must be restored to perfect health again.

To Destroy the Aphis without Tobacco.

If the infested plant is small and short, take three or four *laurel leaves*, beat them all over with a hammer so as to thoroughly bruise them, then place them round or under the plant, and cover; a bell-glass does best.

Let all remain closed for a few hours, and the aphides will be found dead, each hanging by its proboscis only.

If this process is repeated within a day or two to make sure, the plant will be perfectly freed, and in some cases is not again attacked.

This way of killing aphides is particularly acceptable to those who *do not like tobacco-smoke;* all danger arising from an overdose of it to a very tender plant is avoided, and the laurel is so generally grown it must be almost everywhere near at hand.

Tobacco Powder

is an excellent preparation, and is applied by means of a puff when the foliage is damp. It may also be applied by a common tin box with a perforated lid.

The plants infested with the green fly should be dusted with the powder in such a manner that every fly receives its share. The powder must be washed off again with the syringe in about twenty-four hours after its application, to prevent its injuring the foliage.

Quassia Tea.

A good insect remedy may be made by steeping about two ounces of quassia chips in a gallon of hot water. This is very destructive to green fly if the plants are immersed in it.

Geihurl's Compound, an insecticide, is also very useful.

A New Way of Overcoming the Green Fly in Plant-cases.

"Much the easiest and completest way of keeping these sap-stealing and destructive vermin in check in crowded plant-cases is to use the fumes of tobacco. These will penetrate every crevice and reach every hidden aphis without the handling of a pot or a plant, requiring only the use of a good syringe to shower and wash the foliage after the fumigation.

"But in a small case it is quite difficult to get up smoke of sufficient density to be effective, without evolving a damaging amount of heat from the coals which it is necessary to use—as a few coals will not sustain fire enough without flame, which is deadly to the plants. And smoke from a fumigating bellows is not sure to reach every insect, but *is* sure to annoy the

HOW TO DESTROY INSECTS. 11

operator and pervade the room with the unpleasant odors of the burning weed. After two or three victories, bad as defeats, in campaigning against these marauders in the recesses of a plant-case, I caught a happy suggestion about 'touch' which opened the way to full success by so simple and so beautiful an operation that I now almost sigh for more aphides to conquer.

"I made some touch-paper by soaking soft, felt-like wrapping-paper, or the thinner sort of blotting-paper, in a solution of saltpetre, and then allowing it to dry. Taking a strip of this, three or four inches wide and twice as long, strewing shreds of tobacco all over it, and rolling it up from one end into the shape of a giant cigar-stump or a tiny rolly-poly, I had a quasi-cartridge, one of which proves sufficient to destroy every aphis in a 6 by 3 feet window-case. A bit of wire serves to hold it together and to hang it by, and there is nothing more to do but to touch it with a light and to close the window, laying wet strips of paper on the joint, if necessary, to keep all smoke out of the room. The fumes pour incessantly and copiously from the ends of the cylinder, rise to the glass, and then fall cool among the foliage—sure asphyxiation to every one of the robbers.

"This is a peculiarly eligible method for a small case; but in a large plant-house hot coals can be used in sufficient quantity to maintain dense fumes for half an hour, if desired, without risk of burning the plants.

"W."

Persian Insect Powder.

A small quantity of this added to a solution of *whale-oil soap* and *hellebore* will destroy the green fly, and applied with a syringe will keep all rose-bushes free from insects.

Another Method.

Take two ounces of Persian Insecticide, dissolved in one-fourth of a pint of spirits and diluted in ten gallons of water. Two or three applications at intervals of every two or three days will destroy all insects.

Carbolic Soap for Green Fly.

An experiment with this in killing insects on house-plants was made by an editor of a horticultural journal, with notes and results as follows:

"The *green fly* is, as everybody knows, a great pest, and one not readily destroyed, except by fumigating with tobacco, not always very agreeable.

"My first experiment with the *carbolic soap* was a decided success, operating upon two hundred roses just in bloom and it was conducted as follows: Into a pail of warm water I put a lump of soap the size of a small hen's egg. The soap was cut up into small pieces, and the water agitated until it was all dissolved, forming a warm suds.

"The water should not be too hot, but if not above 120° or thereabouts it will do no harm. Into this suds

HOW TO DESTROY INSECTS. 13

each rose-bush was plunged (holding the pot inverted in the hand), and kept there about a half-minute. After plunging, the plants were set aside for a few minutes, then dipped in the same way into clean water, shaking them about thoroughly, washing the leaves, and then returned to their former place in the house.

"Whether it was the soap or the warm water that killed the green fly I will not say, but there is one thing certain—they are all dead."

Hot Water

will destroy aphis instantly, without injury to the plant, if not too hot.

The maximum temperature may be as high as 150° Fahrenheit without any fear whatever, excepting upon very tender plants.

As a general rule, *moisture* is death to insects which infest conservatory and window plants.

While using hot water invert the pot, and hold the earth from falling out with both hands under it, and dip the whole of the top of the plant into water heated as high as 150°.

Tobacco-smoke

is a certain cure. Put in a common flower-pot saucer a few shavings; on these, after you have set fire to them, a small handful of tobacco-stems or leaves previously dampened; place it close to the plant, in a room not in use; cover the plant and saucer of tobacco with a cone made of newspaper, and smoke for fifteen or twenty minutes or less—it depends on the insects and the size of the plant. If any of the aphis are found lying on the earth of the pot, they should be removed and destroyed, or they will recover and return to their former haunts.

Fumigating.

The following device, so far as the production of smoke is concerned, is very satisfactory.

A common tin box, such as dry mustard is sold in, is taken to the tinman, who cuts a hole about half an inch across in the bottom, and solders on a tapering tube something like the nozzle of an oil-can. In the cover of the box he cuts another hole, and solders on a tube flaring slightly outward, of a size to fit over the nozzle of a pair of bellows.

The whole machine looks like one of the affairs which dealers in magic cockroach-powders sell for the purpose of blowing the powder into cracks and crannies. The box is filled with tobacco, and a live coal inserted just under the cover. The tube is then placed on the bellows and the latter put in operation. The result will be a smoke such as no respectable insect will endure for a moment.

Frame of Glazed Cloth.—It is quite practicable to smoke plants, both in doors and out, by using a light frame covered with glazed cloth or other reasonably smoke-proof material. This is made large enough to put bodily over the bush. The nozzle of the smoke-bellows may then be introduced through a suitable aperture, and in a few minutes, or seconds, the smoke inside will be almost thick enough to cut with a knife.

Cloth Roll.—" My way of fumigating plants with tobacco is to take a long, narrow strip of cloth and spread it out; sprinkle tobacco the whole length, then roll tightly, place on a stove-cover or an old plate under the flower-stand, light the roll, and close all doors. It generally proves effectual. M. C. A."

Tobacco in Small Dish.—" Put coarse stems, smoking-tobacco, or cigar-ends on coals in a small dish, and hold it under the plants, over which a newspaper should be thrown to confine the smoke among them until the lice are stupefied; then shake the plants thoroughly, and sweep away all the insects which fall from them. After that sprinkle them thoroughly, taking care to wet the leaves below as well as above."

Another Way of Fumigating.—A gardener in the Hull Botanical Garden of London adopts this method to clean green flies that infest his house-plants:

" Lay the plant on its side in a wash-tub, throw over it a damp towel, or, better, *a bit of glazed calico lining*, and then, through an opening at the bottom, have your husband insert the end of a pipe, and through it let him blow tobacco-smoke until the plant gets a good fumigation. The flies will be found at the bottom of the tub when the operation is finished.

"The plants should be perfectly dry when the operation is performed, but, if a towel is used, it should be freshly washed and wrung out before using, and be without holes. The pipe-stem should reach to the bottom of the tub.

"Be careful when a number of plants are in flower in a greenhouse or conservatory; tobacco-smoke will spoil the flowers."

Other Ways of Fumigation.—Place the plants under a barrel, together with a dish of burning tobacco-stems and leaves, and the smoking will be effectual, closing the career of *aphis, mealy bug, green fly, and brown scale.*

The smoke will be strong enough to suffocate human beings; and the plants even, on being confined in it for an hour, will look pitiful enough, but washing with clean water will enliven them quickly.

Submerging.—Another cultivator prepares a quantity of warm suds in a large, deep vessel, a bathing-tub or something similar, then covers the surface of the soil in the pot with a circular piece of pasteboard fastened on with a stout cloth bandage to prevent dislodgment of the soil by the water, and lays the pot lengthwise therein. Every part of the plant must be completely submerged and remain thus half an hour. Except in the worst cases this effects a cure.

THE MEALY BUG.

The mealy bug is a very annoying insect; it appears like a white mealy spot, not more than one-third as large as a lady-bug, and infests the crotchets of smooth-barked plants, and also gets into the cracks of the bark of rough-barked plants; here it hatches its nests of young ones. The best way to destroy it is to brush the stems with an old tooth-brush dipped into the strongest soap-suds you can make, with a little soot added to the water, and then give the plants a good sprinkling; it can be scraped off with the finger-nails, but the process is not an agreeable one.

S. O. J.

Let it once get a foothold, and it is very difficult to get rid of it.

They can also be kept down by frequent syringing with warm, greasy water, to which a little sulphur should be added; but if full-grown, they should be picked off by the hand or a small, sharp-pointed stick.

Alcohol is sure death to the mealy bug. It can be removed from thousands of the most delicate plants, without a particle of injury, by simply applying frequently, for a few weeks, alcohol diluted with *five per cent.* of water.

The most convenient way to use it is by a fine brush put through the cork of a wide-mouthed bottle.

Kerosene may sometimes be used, as appears by the

testimony of an Illinois window-gardener: "For more than a year I have used kerosene to destroy *mealy bug* and *scale louse,* and have found it a most convenient and effectual remedy. I apply it to the backs of the insects with a feather and brush lightly around the axils of the leaves infected, and I have not found any injurious effects of its use upon the most tender plants."

Powdered white hellebore and *whale-oil soap,* dissolved and sprinkled through any sprinkler, will do the work effectually.

THE SCALE.

THE scale or shield louse is a very troublesome pest. While young they move about freely, but as they get older they fix themselves permanently upon the underside of the leaves or stems, and by a secretion from the body a scale is produced, under the cover of which the insect lives, lays its eggs, and multiplies. These scales are found more particularly upon oleanders, azaleas, camellias, pine-apples, roses, cactus, palms.

The most effectual remedy is to wash and sprinkle the plant with a solution of *Persian Insecticide* or *Girkurt Compound.*

Rub the infected parts with the hand, or pick or scrape them off. Dip twice as many times as for the red spider, in solutions specially intended for that insect, particularly that of soft soap.

White hellebore and soap will clear this pest. One application, if thorough, will be sufficient, although a second application two or three weeks after may be necessary to dispose of a new generation.

SLUGS ON BEGONIAS.

SLUGS are occasionally seen eating large holes or notches in the leaves of all succulents and begonias, making them unsalable and unsightly. They usually feed during the night.

The best mode of ridding the house of these is to cut potatoes, turnips, or some other fleshy vegetable in halves, when they will gather upon them and are easily destroyed.

BLACK ANTS ON PEONIES.

SPRINKLE guano on them, or around their haunts.

WOOD-LICE.

WASH off with strong soap-suds, or use a tooth-brush with bristles cut short, or dip a fine brush in kerosene or alcohol and touch them.

WHITE WORMS.

These white worms, which infest occasionally all soils where plants are kept in pots, may be removed as follows:

Lime-water may be sprinkled over the soil, or a little slaked lime may be sprinkled also on the earth and in the saucer of the pot.

Lime-water may easily be made by slaking a large piece of lime in a pail of cold water, letting it settle, and then bottling for use. Give each pot a tablespoonful twice a week.

EARTH-WORMS IN THE SOIL OF POTS OR LAWN.

a. Take corrosive sublimate, one ounce; common salt, one tablespoonful; boiling water, one pint. Stir till dissolved. Pour the mixture into nine gallons of rain-water, and water the lawn or the soil in flower-pots wherever the worms are to be found.

Lime-water for Worms.

b. A cultivator says: " I have always had good success by using lime-water in the proportion of one pound of lime to four gallons of water. Let it stand over night till perfectly clear; wet the earth but not the plant. I have never needed to use it more than twice, and seldom but once."

HOW TO DESTROY INSECTS. 21

For small quantities, dissolve a lump of unslacked lime, as large as an English walnut, to a quart of water.

c. Another preparation, very good, is one ounce of pulverized *carbonate of ammonia* to one gallon of water.

d. Small bits of *camphor,* dug in the earth among the roots of pot-plants, will effectually destroy earth-worms. Has proved a complete success in many trials.

e. Take a turnip, cut in pieces, and place on the earth at night; in the morning the worms will be at breakfast on the turnip. Remove and kill.

f. Baking the earth in an oven will kill all animal or insect life if other remedies prove unsuccessful. This never fails, while with liquid remedies some will be successful, others unfortunate.

One cultivator observed that in baking the earth it burnt a little, and she noticed that her plants never did better; the petunias and pelargoniums that had been repotted in it were splendid in growth and perfectly gorgeous in color.

g. Repot plants in fresh soil, if you do not wish to take the trouble of other methods of destroying the worms.

h. An English lady flower-lover found that the water the family potatoes were boiled in was a sure cure for worms; put it cold or warm on the earth. It is a very simple remedy, and others have tried it with success.

i. Sprinkle wood-ashes over the tops of the crocks, and also over the surface of the earth.

f. Put your plants into saucers filled with boiling hot water; the heat will cause the tiny mites to ascend to the surface; then pour warm water upon the soil, washing off every worm you can see by holding the pot so as to let them run off. Now scatter red pepper thickly over the surface, and the worms will not trouble you much.

Worms in Pots.

a. A lady cultivator has destroyed these by weakening ammonia with water and pouring around the roots of the plants. Put one ounce of ammonia into one gallon of warm water, and water the plants with it once a week; they will be free from the worms and be beautiful and green.

b. A successful way is to remove the plant, wash its roots in warm water; let it remain in water till the pot is refilled with earth well heated, so as to kill all the worms or eggs that may be laid within the soil. Wash the pot in water warm enough to kill all that may adhere to it.

c. Take fine-cut tobacco, spread a thin layer on top of the earth around the plant when the earth is dry, then water freely; repeat if needed and first application is not thorough.

d. Pour a solution of *tannic acid* around the plant and the worms will be brought to the surface, when they can be easily destroyed.

Worms in Flower-pots.

A cultivator, who had tried salt and lime-water on pot-plants and soil to rid them of the worms, at last tried another method.

Hot water was turned into the saucers of the pots, and warm wood-ashes spread over the surface of the earth and dug in with a hair-pin. The insects were driven away, and the potash was good for the plants.

Wire-Worms.

Rape-cake placed about an inch underground will attract them, and, burying themselves in it, they are easily taken out. This is more effectual to attract them than potato.

Wire-Worms in Pots.

To kill wire-worms in pots use salt, sprinkled over the soil, or a diluted solution, not strong.

The most effectual way, however, is to turn the plants out of the pots and search for the worms.

GRUBS IN POTS.

The best way of dealing with soil infected with grub is to expose it to a fierce heat before using it. For example, it may be put in the oven for a few hours.

Most preparations of a liquid nature, if strong enough

to kill the worms, are also strong enough to do damage to the roots of tender plants.

An always safe way is to turn the plants out of the pots and search for the worms, and replace the ball in the pot again.

OLEANDER BUGS.

To destroy the little bugs that come on the oleander take a piece of lime the size of a hen's egg and dissolve it in about two quarts of water, and wash the stock and branches of the tree.

PLANT-LICE.

Take three and a half ounces *quassia chips* ; add five drachms *Stavesacre seeds*, in powder ; place in seven pints of water, and boil down to five pints. When cooled the strained liquid is ready for use, either in a watering-pot or syringe.

To Kill Green Lice on Flowers.

Take wood-soot or coal-ashes ; where the soot has burnt in the chimney, sprinkle on before a rain, make a tea of it, and water them.

This was tried for three years in a window garden of two hundred plants, and with great success.

FLIES.

Flies do not in general injure house-plants, but any fly, friendly or deadly, may be removed by liberally sprinkling weakened ammonia-water.

SNAILS.

Snails are sometimes met with. A little air-slacked lime thrown on the places they infest is the best preventive against their ravages.

Snails and Ants in Ferneries.

Cut potatoes or yellow turnips in halves, scoop out the pieces, and lay them in the fernery. The slugs and snails will go to them, and are easily caught.

Sprinkle a little fine sugar through a dry, coarse sponge; the ants will go into the sponge, and are easily destroyed by putting the sponge in hot water.

SCALE ON IVY.

Scrape off the scale with a fine knife, being careful not to wound the bark of the plant. This is the only efficacious thing, as even a faithful washing with a stiff brush and water will not answer.

INSECT ENEMIES OF THE ROSE.

Rose-slugs.

The body of the slug is about one quarter of an inch long, green and soft like jelly. Slugs eat the upper surface of the leaf, leaving the veins and skin underneath untouched.

They are most troublesome in June, and frequently reappear in August.

They increase very rapidly, and will destroy the foliage of the largest bushes in a few hours.

The following are remedies used by various florists:

a. Take *white hellebore powder*, mix with water, and sprinkle over them.

b. Dust the plants thoroughly with *powdered lime*, *plaster-of-paris*, or *ashes*.

c. Even *road* dust may be used instead of lime, and be as efficacious; repeat vigorously as often as may be required.

d. Sprinkle the plants thoroughly with a strong suds made of *soft soap*.

e. Whale-oil soap, whenever it can be obtained, the best of special insecticides. It is a powerful enemy of all insect life, and is now for sale at all agricultural stores. Use one pound dissolved in eight gallons of water, or a quarter of a pound to two pails of water; applied by means of a syringe every evening for a week, it effectually destroys all trace of the nuisance.

HOW TO DESTROY INSECTS. 27

f. Another useful article for the destruction of rose-slugs, and other insect enemies of the rose or other garden plants, is found in the *Persian Powder*, sold by most florists.

The powder should be applied three times to the rose-bushes before the buds appear, for after the buds have grown the powder mars the bud and the leaves.

g. Sprinkle sulphur on the rose-bushes early, when the dew is on.

h. Paris green. A correspondent of the *Floral Cabinet* used this remedy for two years with the best success. "A small tablespoonful was mixed in a pailful of water, and applied with a garden water-pot. If used when the slugs first make their appearance, they can be wholly exterminated before flowers or foliage are at all injured. Last year we applied it to some very choice roses, and in twenty-four hours after not a slug could be found."

i. Take one ounce of carbonate of ammonia, dissolved in a pailful of water, and then sprinkle the plants.

Rose-bugs.

A very determined and obstinate enemy. It comes without premonition, flies directly into the fresh-opening bud, and burrows a home in the middle of the blossoms of your most beautiful and carefully cherished floral treasure, and is as voracious as a tobacco-worm.

None of the usual insect enemies conquer him, so the war must be waged by hand.

Hand-picking is the only efficacious remedy. This is slow but sure. Begin early in the morning; pick or brush them into a vessel containing boiling water, after which gather them together and burn them.

Air-slacked lime scattered over the bushes while wet with dew in the early morning is usually a sufficient protection from them.

Red Spider.

This appears more often on window plants than those out of doors. It is difficult to see when it first appears, unless it is in considerable numbers, and may be detected by the browned or deadened appearance of the leaves.

Moisture is sure death to it.

Sprinkle or wash with water frequently. If the plants are badly attacked, sponge the under side of the leaves daily.

Green Fly.

If the aphis or green fly attack roses, an application of *tobacco-water* will usually make an end of them, or finely-powdered tobacco may be sprinkled on them from an old pepper-box.

The green fly attacks the young shoots, and will first be found at the extremities of the branches. It feeds

HOW TO DESTROY INSECTS. 29

on the juices of the plant, and will soon sicken and starve a whole bush.

The usual application of tobacco-smoke for half an hour under a barrel will always kill them completely.

Mildew on Roses.

This is manifested by a whitish-looking mould or dust on the plants.

If plants are growing out of doors, stir the soil frequently. If plants are growing in doors, sprinkle a fine dusting of flour of sulphur over the whole plant. In general sulphur will prove a good antidote to mildew on any plant.

The Yellows.

If the leaves of your rose-bush turn yellow from any cause, and it looks unhealthy, take up in the morning, put in milk-warm water, and carefully wash the roots; this will be found very beneficial; it should remain in water, sufficient to cover the roots, until evening, and, after mellowing the soil, again set it out; shield from the sun a few days.

A weak decoction of soot-water is excellent; but it must be applied very weak and not too frequently.

Paris Green.

A remedy is used by some with great care, as follows for all insect enemies of all plants:

Mix paris green and water in the proportion of one

ounce to three gallons of water. Sprinkle over the plants with a small broom.

It is sure destruction to all insects that *eat leaves*, but it is a question whether it is not so dangerous as to be needful of great care to handle with safety, as it is poisonous also to human beings. Keep the mixture well stirred, as the green settles rapidly.

Scotch Snuff.

A lady who generally keeps off all her insects by frequent sprinkling says: "Where any do dare to intrude, they get *Scotch snuff* to the right of them, Scotch snuff to the left of them, and Scotch snuff all around them, till the air, to them, is thick with Scotch snuff, and they probably end their existence by sneezing their little heads off. This I allow to remain a day or two before sprinkling again."

Rose-grubs.

If there are any grubs in stems of roses run a fine wire into their holes and kill them.

Rose-slugs.

Add a teaspoonful of powdered white hellebore to two gallons of boiling water. Apply, when cold, in a fine spray, bending the tops over so as to reach the under surface of the leaves. One application is usually sufficient.

HOW TO DESTROY INSECTS. 31

Rose-slugs—Wood-ashes.

An experienced cultivator, after trying *picking off* the slugs by hand and burning them, also various remedies, such as *hellebore, paris green*, etc., with indifferent success, at last found nothing that would so thoroughly destroy rose-slugs as *wood-ashes*.

The ashes must be sifted on early in the morning, while the leaves are damp, the branches being turned over carefully, so that the under sides of the leaves, to which the young slug clings, may get their share of the siftings.

If the night has been dewless, in order to make the work thorough first sprinkle the bushes, and the ashes will then cling to the slugs, to their utter destruction. This may be repeated without injury to the roses, as often as the pests make their appearance.

VARIOUS HINTS AND REMEDIES FOR DESTROYING INSECTS.

Kerosene, or Coal-oil, as a Remedy for Insects.

A LADY cultivator uses one tablespoonful of kerosene oil mixed with one pail of water, and syringes the plants occasionally, being careful not to allow much of the water to get upon the soil in the pot.

Another lady cultivator dips a little brush in coal-oil, touches with it all insects that can be reached, and finds it sure death. However, if the oil touches the plants it will destroy them also.

Alum-water for Destroying House Insects, etc.

No insect which usually infests the house, and crawls over the floors or woodwork, can live under the application of *hot alum-water.*

It will destroy *red* and *black ants, cockroaches, spiders, chintz-bugs,* and all the crawling pests that infest the house.

Take two pounds of alum and dissolve it in three or four quarts of boiling water; let it stand on the fire until the alum is all melted, then apply it with a brush, while nearly boiling hot, to every joint and crevice in your closets, bedsteads, pantry shelves, and the like.

Brush the crevices in the floor of the skirting or mopboards, if you suspect that they harbor vermin. If in whitewashing a ceiling plenty of alum is added to the lime, it will also serve to keep insects at a distance.

Cockroaches will flee paint which has been washed in cool alum-water.

How to use Tobacco-water.

The most effectual way to use tobacco-water is as follows: Procure the strongest shag, and make an infusion by pouring upon it boiling water.

The whole quantity of water required may be applied

HOW TO DESTROY INSECTS.

in the first instance on a portion only, adding the remainder cold some time afterwards.

A safe rule for plants of every kind is to allow *half a gallon of water to every ounce of tobacco.*

The tobacco may be infused a second time and the liquid added to the first; the second infusion should be not more than a quart of water to every ounce of tobacco. Plants with leathery leaves will bear stronger doses than plants with thin, papery leaves, and the best time to use the liquid is in the afternoon or evening.

Small plants are best cleansed by dipping them.

Have ready a vessel large enough for the purpose filled with tobacco-water. Take hold of the pot with one hand, and place the fingers of the other over the soil in just the same manner as if about to turn the plant out of the pot. In this way dip the plant head downwards into the liquid, and hold it there a few seconds.

If there are many to be operated on, it would be well to have the liquid in a trough and some pieces of wood laid across; on the pieces of wood the edges of the pots could rest, and, beginning at one end, the plants could be turned over with their heads in the liquid, and remain so till the trough is filled, which, of course, would occupy but a brief space of time.

When taken out of the bath the plants should be laid on their side to drain, and then be well syringed with pure, soft water.

This method of proceeding entirely prevents the absorption by the soil in the pots of any of the tobacco-water, which would injure the roots, and it moreover ensures the complete wetting of the under sides of the leaves. The liquid should always, if possible, be used tepid, and it is then more effectual than when used quite cold. Indeed, it may be used as hot as the hand will bear it comfortably without injury to the plants.

An Easy Way of Making Tobacco-tea.

A lady famous for her success in splendid, healthy plants gives her secret as follows:

"Every two weeks all the winter I would take a handful of tobacco-stems and steep them by pouring boiling water over them until it looked like strong tea; then, when the tea cooled enough for the hand to bear, I poured it over the plants. Sometimes the leaves would wilt for a few moments, and then straighten out and have that bright, fresh look they have in summer after a shower. Then I would weaken the tea a little more and wet the ground in the pots, and I have no red spider or green fly."

How to use Whale-oil Soap.

Mix *whale-oil soap and sulphur* together in the proportion of *one ounce* of the former and half an ounce of the latter to a gallon of water, and give the plants a good washing while at rest. It will prove most excellent as a *preventive* of the ravages of *thrips* and *red* spider, which, if not kept in check, are troublesome when the plants are in full growth, and weaken them much by causing the leaves to turn a sickly color and fall off, so that the flowers are neither so plentiful nor so fine as on a vigorous, healthy plant.

To use it successfully lay the plant over a tub in such a way that the shoots, which are very brittle, do not get broken, and with a powerful syringe dash the mixture thoroughly into every joint, and it usually keeps the plants clean for the season.

The plants are turned on the side to wet the under sides of the leaves, which is the general hiding-place for insects, and also to prevent the water from dropping on the soil in the pots; for, although not deleterious in itself, it chokes the pores of the soil and prevents the water from passing freely.

It is not advisable to use this or any other mixture on the foliage while the growth is young and tender, and certainly not when in flower.

The foliage of azaleas is very easily injured when in a young state, and requires great care if necessary to fumigate with tobacco at any time; but if the plants are clean before flowering, a free use of the hose or syringe each day while growing is usually sufficient to keep insects in check.

To Restore Frost-bitten Plants.

If by any accident plants become frost-bitten, they may be restored by immersing them immediately, while they are stiff, in cold water, and keeping them thus in a darkened room for an hour or two, or placing them in the cellar for a night or so.

White Spots on Window-sills.

A white spot is often made on a painted window-sill by allowing flower-pots to set long thereon. To remedy this take fine wood-ashes, rub the spot, then wash off with clean water.

NOTES AND FLORAL EXPERIENCES
Of Cultivators in Destroying Insects and Using Remedies.

Plant Parasites.

THE struggle with parasites is the plant-lover's chief trial, and the microscope is a good assistant. The *green louse* is a brilliant, bright-eyed animal under the microscope, but his brilliancy will hardly atone for his enormous appetite. *Red spiders* are active little workers and easily discovered. They will not flourish under frequent cold baths, while the *aphides* will not yield to anything but hot water and the heavy hand of fate. They are to be brushed off the plants; then, unless boiling water is poured over them (in the sink), they can be seen walking tip-toe through the cold water in pursuit of vegetation once more; eternal vigilance can keep them decimated, and plants most infested should be put in cooler rooms. The *slug* is more insidious;

HOW TO DESTROY INSECTS. 37

he builds a stationary house, then sallies forth to destroy. Too small to be detected by the naked eye, the microscope shows minute red, animated bodies with several legs, not unlike the red spider; turn his house upside down with a pin, and it appears like a nest full of squirming chickens. These houses, or *scales*, appear on the leaves, stems, and stalks of ivies, on rose-stalks, and I have seen them on carnations, bouvardias, and the ivy-leaved pelargoniums; when they are numerous it may well be supposed that the inhabitants are present in vast numbers. A sticky, gummy substance precedes their appearance, which may be noticed in small spatters on leaves and wall-paper; the remedy is *to get them off.* Ivies can be washed with an old tooth-brush most effectually, brushing both sides of the leaves, the stems, and stalks with weak soap-suds; this, if done thoroughly twice a year, will keep a large ivy in good health, even if kept in the house all summer. Smaller ones can be washed oftener with ease. Small ivies should be kept in pots with other plants till a foot or two in length, or even longer; this not only economizes space, but the ivy will have a stronger root and more rapid growth; when large enough to be an ornament it may be given a pot by itself."

Manure-water, Soot-tea, etc.

"Now let us see the ladies kill the insects. One is told that a sprinkling of wood-ashes will kill the tiny worms in her pots and improve the plants. Very true. But she forthwith puts a tablespoonful in each pot and kills her plants. Another is told that liquid manure is beneficial. She drenches plants with a strong, black solution, and then stands aghast at seeing the leaves turn brown and fall off. A third kills plants with ammonia, and a fourth, hearing of the good effects of warm water in winter, scalds her plants as heedlessly as if she expected to have boiled callas and bouvardias for dinner. I once committed my full share of such blunders, but, having plodded my way to universal success, hope that all our 'sisters' may, in this enlightened age, attain the same at less expense. I once top-dressed my dahlias with fresh stable-manure (taking care not to let it touch the stem), and it made them bloom beautifully, keeping the ground moist and gradually enriching it. Next year I applied hen-manure in the same way, and it 'burnt up' the plants. I would not recommend the latter as a liquid manure. A weak solution of cow-manure (color of weak coffee) is safer and better than anything else. I have found that *soot and wood-ashes combined* will cure every ill that the royal rose is heir to. If it is covered with insects, if the leaves look brown and spotted, if it is doing badly in any way, just sprinkle it well with water and dust it freely with soot and ashes mixed in equal proportions. If the rose is planted out, let it remain until the next rain washes it off. If potted let it stay on for four or five days.

HOW TO DESTROY INSECTS. 39

"I have seen this application change the color of a dull, sickly pink rose into a most lovely and vivid red. If a rose seems to be dying, or much injured by a hard winter, don't give it up until you have tried watering it once a week with soot-tea, made by boiling one light pint of soot in twelve of water. This is also excellent for fuchsias. If the leaves of your heliotrope are brown and rusty on the edges, remove the surface soil carefully and replace it with fresh dirt which has a good deal of charcoal and one teaspoonful of soot mixed with it, and the good result will soon be apparent. Now for the grand 'Masonic' secret of success. Always top-dress your plants if they seem sickly or refuse to bloom, but don't repot them every time they seem to be doing badly. Top-dressing has as good an effect as 'change of air' with human invalids, but too frequent repotting is truly said to be the bane of plant-culture."

Scale-louse, Mealy-bug, etc.

"I have had something to do with the above-mentioned intruders during the past summer. These disgusting creatures were introduced to my notice by a myrtle and two bouvardias (pink and white) received from the greenhouse some months ago. I wondered why my myrtle grew so slowly, and one day, on giving it a more loving look than usual, I discovered it was literally covered with little brown scales, the midribs and axil of every leaf, and all along the woody stem, till every joint looked swollen. I immediately thought of the scale-louse I had read of, so I concluded this was the pest and went to work. I put the pot on a paper, and with a dull penknife carefully scraped every stem and leaf till they fell down thick on the paper, which I burned; then, with an old tooth-brush, I scrubbed the entire plant with soapsuds with ammonia in it, and have repeated this operation three times within as many weeks, and my myrtle, even in this short time, shows a change; it is putting out tiny shoots all over, and every little glossy leaf looks bright and healthy now. I know it thanked me for those scrubbings.

"In many places one would scarcely detect the scale-louse, it looks so much like the bark, but a touch with the point of your penknife will soon tell you if it is there. My pink bouvardia I treated the same way; and it is also flourishing. The white bouvardia (*Jasminoides*) had the mealy-bug on it, and before I had observed it they had infested my Vinca Harrisonia, but constant watching has freed them both from this pest. One day you will see some white powdery-looking stuff, and the next, perhaps, a snug nest of young mealybugs; they increase rapidly, as it seems to me all enemies of plant-life do. I find it best to look over all plants from the greenhouse, for there is almost always some enemy hiding around, and one infested plant will soon spread through a collection, and give more work of the kind than one cares to perform."

The Verbena Rust.

"I could not grow verbenas at all. Some seasons not more than three or four out of a large bed would live; at other times all would persist, notwithstanding my care, in dwindling down into sickly, puny plants, which I could not help feeling were a disgrace to my garden, and have many a time rooted up in sheer despair, preferring an empty bed (for they generally hung on until it was too late for anything else to take their place) to the sight of so many invalids. The disease known as 'black rust' was the foe I had to contend with.

"In vain I tried every remedy I would hear of: had new beds cut in virgin soil, as many gardeners advise, watered with solutions of ammonia, copperas, petroleum, whale-oil soap, etc.; at other times had old rotten compost brought from the woods and duly mixed with sand and well-rotted manure, and when that failed have tried various fertilizers, but with no better success. Every book of acknowledged merit I could find on floriculture I greedily searched in hopes of finding in it some solution of my especial difficulty; none, however, appeared, and I began to think there must be something in the soil or climate of our particular locality against which it was useless for me to strive longer (I had tried plants from a number of different florists, grown both from cuttings and seed), when help came unexpectedly to me from a conversation I had held with a friend some years previously on the subject of raising gooseberries, or rather on the difficulty of doing so satisfactorily, the berries proving so very far inferior, both in size, quality, and flavor, to those raised by our neighbors across the mill-pond. My friend's theory was this: 'That the hot sun shining on the bushes, while still both leaves and fruit are dripping with dew, causes all the mischief; if, therefore, you want no mildew,' said he, 'plant where there is shade from the morning sun, so that the dew may dry gradually from the heat of the atmosphere; manure the soil freely; water, if dry weather, at the roots only, and you will find your gooseberries, after a year or two, will astonish you and all your neighbors.'

"Now, thought I, if this treatment be so good for the gooseberry, why not for the verbena? It will, at any rate, do no harm to try. So once more I sent for verbenas for a bed which was shaded from the east by a terrace; once again I planted my favorites, watered, watched, and waited. I wish some of the readers of the *Cabinet* could have seen that bed about the end of the July following; it was a perfect blaze of glory. No wilted, sickly plants; no black rust! Nothing in the whole garden could compare with it; even passers-by were attracted, and stopped to admire its brilliancy, little thinking how long and how hard its owner had toiled ere she succeeded in making those healthy, strong-looking flowers annual visitors to her garden, where they are now such welcome guests.   ALA"

Thrips and Small Pots.

"If you would get rid of thrips you must rise early. Perhaps you do not know the creatures personally. Allow me to introduce them to you, lest you encounter them unawares. I will tell you what I know about them, though they will hardly keep still long enough for me to give them a critical examination.

"The thrip is a small, white fly; pure white it looks on the leaf, on the under side of which it is usually found. The moment you touch the leaf it is ready to fly into your face, nose, eyes, and all over you.

"The only cure for them is tobacco-smoke. As I cannot apply that remedy I have to take them early in the morning, before they get warmed up enough to make them lively. I took a salvia one morning and plunged it, head foremost, into a tub of water. The vexatious creatures would not drown or be drowned. They rose in myriads out of the water, like a flock of doves. I stirred the water round and round, and came to the conclusion that they were more difficult to kill than a cat, which is said to have nine lives. The method I am now taking to dispose of them is to lift the leaves very gently, in order not to disturb their nap, and to wipe them off with a wet sponge, taking care to kill every one. I hope, by care and perseverance, to rid myself of this pest. They are very troublesome on salvias, lantanas, bouvardias, and roses. If you should be so unfortunate as to be troubled with them, you will find on the under side of your leaves little white specks adhering to the leaves. These I take to be the egg or germ from which the insect is developed, and they must all be washed off carefully.

"MAY'S MIGNONETTE."

Experiments with Salt and Hot Water.

"Every season I have tried some new idea. One season it was salt—so I salted to death some very flourishing carnations and roses. The recipe said a teaspoonful of salt to a small pot. I tried it in a good-sized one, and the leaves fell off from the plants or dried upon the stems; so I learned a lesson not to use salt. Then lime-water was certain death to them. I think the worms in my pots fed upon it, for they increased daily. So I took the matter in hand, and turned boiling water into the saucers of plants that were injured by them. This made an end of all the tiny mites that were in the saucers, and the roots sucked up the bottom heat, and grew in grace and beauty. Then I continued to give them a hot sud every morning, but still the miserable crawlers luxuriated upon the roots of my plants and covered the surface of the pot. So a tablespoonful of warm—*not hot*—wood-ashes was spread over the surface of the pots, and with a hair-pin they were dug into the soil. They exercise a very beneficial effect upon the intruders, who could not enjoy a taste of lye, while the roots of the plants were thankful for

HOW TO DESTROY INSECTS. 45

the potash they contained, and were stimulated into fresh growth by it."

Tobacco for Green Bugs.

"After two years' experience in trying to rid my house-plants of the green insect, I have found that a good method is to get a paper of cut and dry tobacco (such as smokers use for the pipe); spread it about one fourth of an inch deep over the soil in the pot; when this disappears add more. I have succeeded in keeping my plants free altogether by this remedy.

"Mrs. M. M. S."

Green Bugs.

"The little green bugs I have had by the millions, yes, by the trillions, especially on my rose-bushes. I tried everything any one told me of to get rid of them, but nothing had any effect. I sprinkled and dusted and powdered, and powdered and dusted and sprinkled, but the little pests were as 'cute as I, and crawled on the under side of the leaves, where they kept just as dry as the Israelites when they passed through the Red Sea. A florist told me to sprinkle them with tobacco-water, but finding sprinkling did no good, I made Baptists of them and gave them a '*dip;*' and not only a dip, but I took a sponge and washed both sides of every leaf on every plant that had a bug on it with strong tobacco-water, and, hurrah! Hail Columbia! that did the business, for I have not seen four bugs in the whole garden since. It was a very tedious job, but it paid. After I washed each plant I poured some of the water around the roots. EL MINA."

Bugs—Cold Water.

"I this winter have followed the practice of a greenhouse proprietor. I bought a plant that was covered with buds and flowers. He said he never had bugs of any description, and his practice was to open the faucet and let the water run *directly* on to the buds and leaves, and in that way give them a thorough washing *once a week*. I thought it was harsh treatment for anything always considered so delicate, but thought I would try it first on some plants about which I should not feel so disappointed if it killed them. They looked so much better for it that after a few days I ventured to put the others to the same test, and have continued to do so *once a week*, no matter *how cold* the weather, and they have well paid me for the trouble in their improved appearance. Of course care must be taken not to let the water run on to the roots. MRS. H. S. H."

Green Bugs again.

"On taking my plants to the kitchen a few days since for their weekly ablutions, I discovered a fine bouvardia literally alive with these disagreeable creatures. Now, in previous years I have succeeded in destroying the insect with tobacco, applied variously, but then the plants died also; so I concluded to prepare some strong soap-suds; then I thoroughly washed the leaves with a cloth and plunged the entire plant under water. At night I again examined my plant, and lo! it was as thickly covered as before; indeed, I believe the insects enjoyed a good bath, and perhaps considered it a special preservative treatment administered for their own benefit. I became so much interested in this amphibious creature that I concluded to examine it under the microscope. I gently raised one of them on the end of my finger and placed it under the glass, when oh! horrible, it changed from an inoffensive green mite to a creature the size of a toad, with two most villanous, opaque-looking eyes prominent on each side of its head, resembling very much the toad's, but its body was beautifully marked with dark rings. On each side were attached three legs, which were jointed and furnished at the end with two claws, giving the foot the shape of a hook. From each side of its head appeared two long propellers (thus I term them, for they seemed to be used in guiding the body). In the rear were two more—I might say legs, but they were stiff and only half the length of the legs, so I concluded they were in some manner connected with the proper engineering of the body.

" The creature seemed frightful; my inclination was to take him up with the tongs and drop him out of the window, but there was my poor plant covered with these vegetable vampires, and how was I to destroy them and at the same time not sacrifice my plant?

"A friend of mine tells me she kills them one by one, but oh! how slow."

Mealy-bugs.
Scene—A Conservatory.

Spectators ensconced in dark corners of the cobweb galleries plotting the destruction of some poor fly. Also, parties of aphis are present, more intent upon chewing geranium leaves than upon witnessing the performances. There may be a toad or two in the pit, but if so they were not sufficiently awake to cheer. Pussy stood in the door winking and purring in anticipation of a good fee in catnip from a pot in one corner.

The performances commenced with the Mealy-bug March, closing with a tragedy, accompanied with the Dead March in Saul.

The instruments used were a tooth-brush and small syringe, winding up with a grand flourish from the watering-pot.

Let me *describe*, not introduce, to you this same mealy-bug. It is by no means an ugly-looking insect. They remind me of guinea-pigs, oval in form, in color white, a silvery white, with sometimes a buff or a pink tinge, as if the pink were seen through gauze, reminding one of those pretty white shells with pink lining. They are disgusting creatures to kill, and are very troublesome on some plants, particularly on bouvardias. I have been fighting them on an ivy geranium for the past two years. They move so unwillingly it is a mystery to me how they get from one plant to another. The Mealy-bug March is a very slow march. I wish to put you on your guard against them. I had frequently read of them, but did not make their acquaintance until about three years ago. At that time I received from a greenhouse two plants of basella rubra, in fine condition apparently. Not suspecting mischief, and being busy, I merely watered the plants when necessary for some little time; but alas! one day, on close examination, I found the stems covered with white insects. I find them on the stems of plants, in the axils of the leaves, on the under and sometimes on the upper sides of the leaves. They infest bouvardias, coleus, cissus, discolor, and one of my ivy geraniums. I cannot smoke them, and I do not like to use tobacco soap or water, as I think it poisons me, so I persevere in washing and brushing. The best way to do is to "look out for the engine before it comes." Sometimes they are not larger than a small pin-head, and sometimes are half as large as a water-bug. Look out for all little white specks on your plants, for they often contain the germ of a troublesome insect.

If a plant from a greenhouse looks fresh and flourishing, do not take it for granted that it is going to be free from insects, but examine it daily, and do not complain of the florist who has sold you the plant, for if you cannot keep half a dozen plants free from vermin how can you expect him to do so with hundreds?

MAY'S MIGNONETTE.

Potash for Ants, etc.

A lady troubled with ants and other insects says:

"Use from one-half to one ounce of *potash* in a pail of water, and give the insects a shower-bath, and they will go without even saying good-by.

"Near plants and roots I do not like to use this alkali, neither do I like to destroy ants, as they are good hunters after still worse insects. Then I use *red pepper*, and create a flight that leaves not a soul behind.

"For or against rats, mice, moles, etc., I also use a paste of potash, and put some of it in their holes or runways where they have to walk. For cleaning trees, shrubs, etc., I use soft-soap mixed with some potash and water, and, with a garden syringe, a good washing cleans every tree, shrub, and plant."

Red Pepper.

A friend has tried red pepper with good results, dusting it over the surface of the soil, and also upon the leaves and branches of plants infested with green spiders and green flies. The pepper does not seem to injure the plants, but in a day or two they should be placed in a tub and receive a good showering of warm water.

In using red pepper it must not be put on by the tea-

HOW TO DESTROY INSECTS. 51

spoonful, but only dusted over the surface through a pepper caster.

A Stimulating Liquid.

"I am using a stimulating liquid composed of sulphate of ammonia, four ounces; nitrate of potash, two ounces; add to them one pint of boiling water; when thoroughly dissolved, cork tightly, and put a teaspoonful of it to every three quarts of warmish water used in watering. A few drops of it added to the water in hyacinth-glasses will stimulate the bulbs to much finer growth and blossoms. This liquid seems to be obnoxious to the small white worms. C. G."

Sulphur.

"I used *sulphur* on my rose-bushes early in the spring; sprinkled them when the dew was on. It destroyed the insects on the foliage; they bloomed beautifully. I tried it on a Jerusalem cherry-tree, for green lice, with good success. *Quassia-bark tea* is excellent for the same purpose."

Lice on Rose-bushes.

"A good way to kill lice on rose-bushes is to take a piece of whale-oil soap about the size of an egg to a gallon of hot water (it dissolves better in hot); then apply with watering-pot or syringe; let it remain on the bushes about ten minutes, then wash off with clear water (for young bushes and for the new foliage make the solution half as strong); repeat about twice during the spring, and you will have fine roses."

Quassia for Rose-bugs, etc.

"The Illinois Horticultural Society recommend quassia as the best medicine for the insects that mutilate rose-bushes and many other garden shrubs. Make a strong tea of quassia-bark—it costs ten or twelve cents a pound wholesale—and drench the bushes. The little pests will not fancy the taste any better than sick children do."

Rose-slug.

"I have tried many remedies (so called) without effect, but for the last two summers I have kept my roses clear of them by the following wash: Two ounces alum, one ounce hellebore, to one gallon water, applied with a syringe, once a week, during the season of the slugs, commencing when the leaves begin to appear.
"Mrs. J. C. O."

"Get white hellebore, one ounce, and dissolve in a pailful of soft, cold water, the colder the better. Take it on a sunny morning after the dew is entirely dried off, put the mixture in a watering-pot, and give the bushes a good showering, throwing it up under the leaves as much as possible, wetting them all over thoroughly. It will not harm the bushes or roses in the least; but, I assure you, the worm that gets his share of the dose will eat rose-leaves no more for ever. Please tell the ladies of this, that they may save those beautiful roses. Mrs. H. F. W."

The *Practical Farmer* says: "We absolutely know, and have proved, that carbolic acid soap-suds, injected over the bush through a common syringe, is an effectual cure for the rose-slugs, and also death to caterpillars."

White Hellebore—" If your readers have been troubled as I have been with the small slug which destroys the leaves of the roses, they will be glad to know that a decoction of white hellebore, sprinkled over the bushes twice, is a successful remedy. I take a quarter of a pound and steep it in a gallon of water, and when cold apply with a whisk-brush. My rose-bushes are looking finely where the application was made, while others are nearly ruined."

Insects on Rose-bushes—Remedy.

" I know one really safe and sure remedy to rid outdoor and indoor rose-bushes of insects of all kinds. It is this: A sufficient quantity of blood-warm water made into suds with common soft or hard soap. Wash the foliage and branches thoroughly, allowing enough drainage through the roots to destroy all insects upon the surface or within the soil, and then carefully rinse the foliage, branches, and roots with blood-warm, clear water. Give pure air, warmth, and light. This is sure and safe. Ami."

Salt for Roses.

"I saw an account in a paper about three years ago of the success of the Shakers at New Lebanon, N. Y., in raising fine foliage and flowers. This the brother in charge attributed to the free use of salt as a top-dressing for the soil of the beds. The salt kills rose insects of every kind, and also improves the health and vigor of the plants. I had been unable, previous to seeing this account, to have a single perfect flower, and as I thought that salt could do no worse than slugs did, I would try it. So to about half a dozen bushes I used a quart of rock-salt, worked into the dirt about three or four inches from the body of the bushes. This was done as soon as I could work the ground in the spring. I had some nice roses, and my bushes grew nearly a foot higher than they ever had before. The next spring I did not work in the salt until the bushes had begun to leave out. This did not prove as successful as the year before; so I think, in order to prevent the ravages of the slug, you must work in the salt as early in the spring as possible, so as to hinder the insect from hatching.

"A. C. F."

SPECIAL FERTILIZERS, WASHES, AND STIMULANTS

For Flowers and House-Plants.

The following has been used with good success in the health of greenhouse plants and out-of-door shrubs and

HOW TO DESTROY INSECTS. 55

trees, as well as indoor plants, in preserving in good health from mildew, scale, red spider, etc.:

Flour of sulphur, two ounces, worked to a paste with a little water; sal-soda, two ounces; cut tobacco, half an ounce; quicklime, the size of a duck's egg; water, one gallon. Boil together and stir for fifteen minutes, and let cool and settle. In using, dilute lightly if plants are tough and hard woods, but dilute much if plants are tender, and then syringe with water after each application.

A Good Wash and Preventive of Insects.

A lady thus describes how she prevents insects from troubling her plants:

"I take one ounce of carbonate of ammonia and a half ounce of sulphuric acid, and mix together (which forms the same as sulphate of ammonia), to which I add one drachm of creosote, and put all into two gallons of rain-water. I then pour into each pot about a gill once a month. This keeps the insects from the roots, besides being a good manure. Once or twice a week I give the plants a thorough drenching with lukewarm water, which keeps them from the leaves, besides washing the dust off the leaves, which is sure to accumulate on all plants kept in the house."

"I read so much about carbonate of ammonia in the *Cabinet* that I procured some and went to showering my plants with it. I can testify that it is not overrated. My plants, after the first bath, showed its good effects. It causes them to look so healthy, and gives them such a lovely green, I would not do without it. Then its good effects do not end here. You may talk about water and cleanliness to keep off the green lice. I have watered, and brushed, and sponged, but they only seemed to come the more, until I commenced showering them with carbonate of ammonia in the water; then they disappeared, and their hateful presence torments me no more."

Epsom Salts

have been used by some amateurs with good success in ridding their plants of insects. Dissolve in water and sprinkle both leaves and soil.

Plaster-of-Paris.

The *green slug, or rose-leaf-eater,* has often been conquered by dusting the bush freely with *plaster-of-paris* early in the morning before sunrise, when the insect is freely at work, and when the foliage is wet with dew to mingle and hold the plaster.

Coal-oil.

Water slightly sprinkled with coal-oil (to give it an odor only) may be used directly on the leaves when bugs or worms are found.

PART II.

INSECTS IN THE GARDEN.

SLUGS.

Pear-slugs.

This insect, which plays such sad havoc with pear-trees, and sometimes with the foliage of plum and cherry-trees, is destroyed in a variety of ways:

1. By taking shovels, and shovelling up the light surface-*dust* of the soil around the tree, and throwing up into the air over the tree, so that in falling it will fall on the upper side of all the leaves of every tree where the slug is eating. The dust falling upon the slugs stops all their pores and breathing apparatus, and in a few minutes or hours they will curl up and fall off dead.

Any description of fine dust, lime, or powder thrown over them is sure death. The surface-dust of the earth is the cheapest, speediest, and most efficacious remedy known.

There must be no delay the moment the slugs are seen; a single day may be enough for the slugs to do incalculable damage, as if any leaves are eaten off a tree it is injured and the next crop is practically ruined.

2. Frequent applications of a mixture of lime, soot, and soap-suds may be made over the trees by means of a garden syringe.

The mixture is made by adding to twelve gallons of cold water one bushel of soot and half a peck of unslacked lime, allowing it to stand one day to settle, after which is added one pound of soft soap dissolved in warm water.

Slugs on Currants.

Take whale-oil soap, a solution of one pound to five gallons of water; sprinkle over the leaves from a watering-pot with a fine hose.

Slugs on Cabbages.

Quicklime dusted on the ground in early morning is a good remedy, but to be effectual it ought to be repeated within an hour, because the slugs have the power of casting their skins, and, after getting rid of the lime, will seek shelter.

Slugs on Cherries, Pears, etc.

Take dust, even road-dust or surface-dust of the garden, and throw over the leaves where the slug is eat-

HOW TO DESTROY INSECTS. 59

ing, and it will adhere to the slimy surface of the insect and choke him, so that he will fall off and die.

All slugs of a slimy nature are killed with dust or oil.

Pear-slug.

Destroy with lime, road-dust, and solution of *white hellebore, quassia, Paris green with water, whale-oil soap, carbolic acid,* or *coal-oil.*

Apply the last very weak or trees will be injured.

The Plum-slug.

Dust the leaves when damp, for several days in succession, either with ashes or road-dust. Another method will be to syringe the trees with suds made of whale-oil soap, two pounds to fifteen gallons of water; this has usually proved very sure.

Dusting with *white hellebore* will kill more surely than either of the other remedies, but is more costly.

Slugs in the Garden.

Gas-tar water, diluted to the color of weak coffee, is an excellent preventive to the ravages of slugs on all garden crops. Apply by night from an ordinary watering-pot, and half the slugs will be killed and the rest much weakened. A second dose after an interval of a week is sufficient to banish them altogether. Slugs may be collected by a little bran placed under some cabbage-leaves, or pieces of bark with the hollow side down, which is also a good trap for wood-lice.

Slugs on Jessamines.

Lay cabbage-leaves around the plant; the slugs will go under them, and can be easily caught and destroyed. Raw potatoes hollowed out serve the same purpose.

CATERPILLARS.

Caterpillars on Berry-bushes or Shrubbery.

Where berry-bushes or shrubbery or young trees are attacked by caterpillars, two dustings of fresh lime over them in the morning, while the leaves are wet with the dew, will kill them all. It will do the same with large trees that are infested, but it is difficult to dust them all over.

Caterpillars on Cabbages.

The fronds of the common *bracken* (*Pteris aquilina*) will drive away the caterpillar. Upon a trial of this by a friend, in less than an hour after the bracken fronds were laid on not a caterpillar was to be seen. Elder leaves are said to be equally efficacious.

Caterpillars on Lawn or Shade Trees.

Daub the stems of the young trees near the leaves with coal-tar every two years. The coal-tar is laid on in a narrow ring around the stem, and a tree thus treated is considered to be safe for two years at least.

Various Recipes for Caterpillars.

Get a quantity of elder leaves, and boil them in as much water as will cover them until the liquor becomes quite black; then clear and cool it, and to every gallon of this liquor add one gallon of tobacco-water. When the trees are quite dry lay it on with a fine rose water-pot, and in about ten minutes the caterpillars will fall off dead.

An excellent remedy consists in a dilute solution (one part in 500) of sulphide of potassium, the infested tree being sprinkled with this substance by means of a small hand-syringe. This method has been successfully used on a large scale in Southern France.

To Destroy Gooseberry Caterpillar.—Take one ounce of hellebore powder and two ounces of *powdered alum*; dilute these first in a small quantity of water, so as to get them thoroughly mixed, then add a gallon of water; apply the mixture to the bushes affected, either by wetting them with a syringe or water-pot on the upper surface of the leaves. The caterpillars will drop off soon after feeding upon the leaves.

Hellebore powder, if dry, will destroy the pests, but cannot be applied as regularly as if diluted. The principal use of the alum-water is to cause it to adhere to the leaves.

One gallon will do for ten to twelve full-sized bushes. Apply this as soon as the insects are observed.

The following is an excellent remedy, which has been used on a large scale in Southern France. Take a dilute solution of *sulphide of potassium*, at the rate of about one part in 500. The infested plants are to be sprinkled with the decoction by means of a garden syringe; the vegetation is not in the least injured by its application.

Hellebore for Caterpillars.—Water the branches affected, and while wet sprinkle some freshly-powdered hellebore over them. In a few minutes the grubs will have made themselves scarce and will not return.

Hemp for Destroying Caterpillars.—A French gardener describes a mode of destroying caterpillars which is quite unusual:

"Many years ago I saw an individual sowing broadcast a coarse, gray powder on beds of cabbages which were almost devoured by legions of caterpillars.

"On enquiry, I found that this was nothing else than the refuse of beaten hemp, and consisted of fragments of the dried and broken leaves, and particularly of the crushed seed-vessels. In half an hour all the caterpillars had fallen down dead as if suffocated."

Probably watering cabbages with water steeped in hemp would be equally beneficial.

Tent-Caterpillars.—1. Kill by hand, with covering of a glove to protect the hand.

2. Apply strong soap-suds.

3. A weak solution of petroleum, applied with a swab or long pole.

4. Plant cherry-trees around all orchards; they will attract all the caterpillars, and the orchard will be un-

HOW TO DESTROY INSECTS. 63

touched. The leaves of cherry-trees are preferred by them to all other fruit-trees.

Coal-tar a Remedy for Caterpillars.—Wherever these get on or under the bark of trees they may be prevented as follows: *Rub the base* of the young trees every two years with coal-tar. A ring of this liquid painted on each tree will have the desired effect, as the caterpillars dread it like the plague.

THE CABBAGE-WORM.

THE green cabbage-worm can be successfully destroyed with *hot water.*

Heat to a temperature of 200° or more, and apply through the rose of a common watering-pot, and the worms will be crucified. A temperature of even a few degrees lower will still destroy the worms and not injure the plants.

This method of destruction is easier and more efficient than the use of salt, carbolate of lime, and other substances usually employed.

A Pennsylvania lady having heard of the noxious influence of *carbolic acid* on various species of insects that infest gardens, she was induced to try its effects upon the *cabbage-worm.*

For this purpose she procured a cake of soap that had been strongly scented with the acid, and, having made a quantity of suds therefrom, she transferred it to a watering-pot, and in the early part of the day, when the green worm is most vigorous in its movements, she gave several garden-plots of cabbage a sprinkling.

These were examined soon after, and a number of dead worms were picked from the leaves. The operation was repeated next day, and, after careful observation, wherever the solution was tried the leaves of the plants were cleared of these pests.

Hot Water for Cabbage-worms.

A gardener who had tried a number of remedies for the cabbage-worm found that sprinkling of red pepper did well, but the best, simplest, cheapest, and most efficient was applying hot water. It may be wrongly applied, to the injury or destruction of the plant, and it may be properly applied, doing no injury and killing the insects. Fill a watering-pot with boiling water and sprinkle the infested leaves only for a second or two. It does its work very quickly on the worms, but the leaves, being thick, are not heated or injured. The older the heads become the less the danger. The operator must practise and spoil a few plants to save the rest. The water, by the time it reaches the plants, will be several degrees below boiling. He must determine by trying how long the hot water will do its work before becoming too cold. At the same time he must ascertain by experiment how long he can contrive to apply the hot water before the leaves are injured by it. A very little time will determine these points.

HOW TO DESTROY INSECTS.

Remedy for Cabbage-worms.

Buckwheat flour, sifted through a sieve early in the evening or in the morning while the dew is on, will effectually eradicate them. Two applications (and often one) will do the work. It is preferable to hellebore, or any other article, for the purpose, and has the advantage of being harmless.

WORMS.

Wire-worms

are very frequent in fields once in grass and just converted over into gardens. Cultivation will eradicate the pest in time, as every time the land is dug the birds will make a feast of the vermin, and the use of lime and salt on the land *when newly dug up* will contrive to thin them.

But there is another very successful way: *sow carrots* in short rows in all the garden-beds occupied with lettuces, onions, and other things that they usually destroy.

As long as they can find their way to a feed of carrots they *will desert everything else*, just as slugs and snails will quit everything else for lettuces.

Sow the carrots quite thick, if broadcast; if in garden-beds, sow at intervals of about two yards across every four-feet bed, and they will catch many vermin, when you can drown them and dispose of them.

Alternate rows of onions, lettuces, etc., with carrots may be sown, and the worms will leave all to go to the carrots for food.

Wire-worms in Turf Land.

A cultivator who for several years had been dreadfully pestered with wire-worms, and his potatoes, turnips, carrots, and other roots were pierced through and through with this pest, had a thought occur to him of an application of spent gas-tar lime.

Two cartloads were obtained from the gas-works, and were mixed with six times as much good soil and manure, each in equal quantities.

This was spread in the ground in November, and dug in a spade deep; then in the spring potatoes and other general crops were planted with stable-manure. Excellent crops were realized that year and afterwards, and not a single wire-worm could be detected after that dressing.

It is very important not to overdose with the gas-lime; dilute it well with soil and manure.

It is also excellent for destroying grubs.

Coal-ashes for Currant-worms.

Currant and gooseberry bushes have been kept free from the currant-worm by mulching heavily with coal-ashes.

The ashes also have another and unexpected value— viz., keeping the ground cool and moist, so that even

English gooseberries will bear heavy crops without sign of mildew.

Worms on Honeysuckle Vines.

Try dusting with fresh lime or hellebore powder; otherwise hand-picking is the only remedy.

Worms on Lawns.

A good way to get rid of these is to take up the turf and relay it on an inch of fine coal-ashes; if the grass is weakly, spread a thin coating of good fine soil on the ashes before laying the turf down.

Raspberry and Currant Worms.

Air-slacked lime is better than ashes, which are often used.

A single application of the lime has been sufficient to rout a large army of worms.

A gardener, setting his red and large grape currants in alternate hills with the black currant, was pleased after trial of three years to find neither infested with the currant-worm, the black currant seeming to prove a perfect preventive; whilst in other portions of his garden, not so planted alternately, the red currants were covered with the worms and were utterly destroyed.

The peculiar odor of the leaf of the *black currant* is particularly disagreeable to many of the insect tribe.

Canker-worms.

1. Syringe with Paris green and water.
2. Catch the moths with rope bands.
3. Surround the trunks of trees with paper bands besmeared with printer's ink.
4. Jar the tree, and the worms will fall down to the ground, where, dropping in straw scattered below, they may be set on fire and all burned up.

Canker-worm Remedy.

Some gardeners have successfully employed Paris green to destroy the canker-worm. The Paris green is mixed with water at about the same rate as for potatoes, or about one tablespoonful to a common-sized water-pail. It is thrown on the trees by means of a hand-forcing pump, through a rose having two or three dozen perforations a tenth of an inch in diameter. The Paris green must of course be kept well stirred to prevent its settling to the bottom of the vessel of water. A convenient method is to place a barrel of water in a wagon, with a pail for making the mixture, and a supply of the poison; and then mix and use as needed while driving through the orchard. The application being made early in the season while the young fruit is quite small, all vestiges are washed off by rains long before the fruit ripens.

Tomato-worms.

Hand-picking is the only effectual remedy.

HOW TO DESTROY INSECTS. 69

The Onion-maggot.

Sow broadcast lime and ashes in the proportion of one of ashes to three or four of lime. If onions show signs of yellows or withering, apply specially in their rows a peck of air-slacked lime to every two hundred feet of length of row.

Currant Measuring Worm.

Use hellebore.

PLANT-LICE.

Currant-louse.

Hellebore is not only the most effectual but, when properly applied, the cheapest remedy known. A good method of using it is to place it in a wide-mouthed jar with a lip around the edge, over which can be tied one or two thicknesses of fine muslin. The hellebore can then be shaken through the muslin directly where it is wanted, with very little waste, and, if of good quality, is certain death to every worm it touches.

Leaf-lice on Fruit-trees.

a. A decoction of tobacco is sometimes successful.

b. A wash composed of three pounds of sal-soda, dissolved in a pailful of water, is another remedy.

c. Three ounces of whale-oil soap to a pailful of water. Apply upon the first indications of the lice. The trees will be injured if much soap is used.

Wood-lice.

If they are so abundant as to be easily reached, pour boiling hot water on them and into their haunts.

They have a great partiality for potatoes, and by scattering these around they will be attracted to them, when the hot water can be vigorously used.

Flower-pots filled with hay have been used, and with such good success that thousands have been killed.

The pots are laid on their sides, and once a day the hay is lifted out of the pots; then shoot the wood-lice into a pail of hot water.

Borer and Bark-louse.

Apply soft-soap and water to all fruit-trees in the first week of June. It not only exterminates the sappers (bark-lice) but banishes the miners (borers).

Scrape the trees early in spring; apply the soft-soap first of June, and again the first of July, and do not forget to adjust the cloth bands by the last of June.

Bark-louse.

This may be destroyed in spring, just after hatching, by the application of alkaline washes, such as lye, soapsuds, or whitewash.

The eggs under the scales may be killed during winter by washing or syringing the trees with coal-oil diluted with three parts of water.

Carbonic acid gas, applied by the use of any vaporizer or fire-extinguisher directly to the trees, has been tried and proved a sure remedy.

Wood-lice

may be destroyed by placing potatoes cut in halves about the plants, which should be examined every day till they disappear.

GRUBS.

Rose-grubs.

Picking off by hand is the only practical remedy when other plans fail or washes have no effect.

Grubs in Flower-gardens and among Bulbs.

Portions of carrots of last year's growth placed an inch below the surface, between the rows of vegetables or of flowers, will draw all the grubs, and they can be taken up now and then and be captured and destroyed.

Gooseberry-grubs.

Brine, tobacco-water, and snuff-water are efficient to kill after the grub has been captured. Hellebore is excellent.

The ground underneath the bushes may be trodden hard, and when the bushes are well shaken they fall, and are easily discovered and killed.

BUGS, BEETLES, AND MOTHS.

Mealy-bugs.

The following remedy has been tried on grape-vines with complete success, being an experiment in a cold grapery in Glasgow, Scotland:

The walls of the houses were given two coatings of lime-wash and glue, adding half a pint of turpentine to each gallon of the mixture.

The rafters and glass were also given at intervals three washings of turpentine, and finally the vines themselves were given a good coating of the following mixture:

Three ounces of soft-soap, three ounces of flower of sulphur, one pint of tobacco-water, two wineglassfuls of turpentine, one gallon of hot water, and clay enough to give it the consistency of paint. The result was healthy vines and a fair crop of grapes, clean and free from mealy-bugs.

Squash-bugs.

Place small pieces of boards, chips, or even green leaves on the ground close around the vines. The bugs will choose these as hiding places during the night. In the morning visit them before their eggs are laid, and gather and destroy them all.

A gardener near Washington, D. C., uses the following remedy:

"To two quarts of gypsum put one tablespoonful of

kerosene-oil; this, sprinkled on the vines when the dew is on, will generally answer for the season. If the bugs return repeat the operation.

"I applied it this season on several thousand hills of melons, cucumbers, etc., after the bugs had commenced operations, and have not since had a vine destroyed. I have used it for several seasons with the same result. This is safer and cheaper than Paris green."

May-bugs.

A successful experiment was tried in Germany for destroying May-bugs on a large scale.

It is known that these bugs always select warm and loose ground for the depositing of their eggs.

Consequently seventeen artificial breeding places were prepared by covering fresh cow-dung with fine earth, and by the middle of July they were found full of eggs or grubs.

After collecting these eggs, etc., they were burnt outside the forest.

Aster-bugs.

Plaster sprinkled over the plants while wet with the dew will put them to flight. It is also an efficacious remedy for the rose-slug.

Quassia-tea will also keep bugs from eating aster flowers.

The Striped Bug.

An Illinois gardener, after using ground or calcined plaster as a remedy for striped bugs, at last improved upon it.

"I used Paris green and calcined plaster, in the proportion of one of the former to fifteen of the latter, as a destroyer of the potato-bug, and also I tried it on squash and melon and cucumber vines, with good success.

"The mixture was dusted on from a common dredging-box, and has proved equally effectual against the Colorado potato-beetle and the striped bug.

"On squashes of the tenderest variety of foliage, like the Hubbard, for instance, and on the hardier, like Cinylin and the winter crookneck, this mixture may be put on while the plant is wet or dry, and does not injure them; and so of musk-melons and cucumbers. But on water-melons the mixture must be used with care."

Cucumber-bug.

Mix hellebore and flour together and scatter over the vine and insects.

Colorado Potato-beetle.

Paris green is sufficient. Mix with very fine ashes in the proportion of twenty to one. Take a tomato-can, with holes in the bottom like a grater and a cover on the top, attach to a long pole, and dust the plants with the powder. A few hours will be sufficient to go over an acre. One or two applications, even when the vines and ground are swarming, will rid the pest thoroughly.

Cucumber-beetle.

Use Paris green in the following proportions: One part green to six parts flour. Apply when the vines are dry, and scatter just a little over the vines. If too much is spread over, the vines are sure to be killed.

Codling-moth.

The following method, suggested by Prof. A. J. Cook, of Agricultural College, Michigan, is the most successful and effectual that can be adopted:

"Place around the trunk of every bearing tree, midway between the ground and branches, a woollen cloth about five inches wide, and sufficiently long to pass around and lap enough to tack. This may be fastened with one or two tacks. I have usually found one placed in the middle to be quite sufficient. The tack should not be driven quite up to the head. Before this cloth band is adjusted the loose bark should be scraped off. This may be done earlier in the season when time will best permit. The bands should be adjusted by June 20. Under these bands the 'worms' will secrete themselves. By July 7 the bands around the earliest apple-trees should be unwound and examined, and the larvæ destroyed. This can be done by passing the bands through a wringer, or by unwinding and crushing with the thumb. Every ten days after the first round—every nine days if the weather is dry and warm—the work should be repeated till the last week of August, and again at the close of the season after the fruit is gathered."

Throw lime on the trees when the dew is on, or just after a rain, and after the fruit is set; a bellows is good for scattering it. The insects will not go where the lime is scattered; they will go away.

ANTS.

Recipes for Destroying Ants.

1. Take four ounces of quassia-chips; boil for ten minutes in a gallon of water, dissolving in the liquid while cooling four ounces of soft-soap.

2. Take one pound of black soap, dissolve it in four gallons of water, and sprinkle the solution through a fine rose over the runs and nests, taking care, however, not to water the roots of the plants with it.

3. The following is a successful poison: ferrocyanide of potassium, one drachm; raspings of quassia, one drachm; sugar in sufficient quantity to form a syrup. The ants are said to devour this greedily and die almost immediately.

4. Fresh Peruvian guano will drive ants from any

spot, however firm a hold they may have obtained on it.

Paraffine and benzoline oil are said to have the same effect.

Turpentine, gas-water, flowers of sulphur, lime-water, a decoction of elder leaves, chloride of lime dissolved in water, and camphor have all been used.

5. For ants in a lawn put a large flower-pot over their hole or place of operations. The ants will build up into the pot, and in a short time it may be lifted up and carried away and dropped into a vessel of water, which will be the end of them.

6. For ants on fruit-trees put a line of gas-tar all around the tree, and that will stop their progress.

7. Ants in flower or garden beds may be destroyed as follows:

Take two ounces of soft-soap, one pound of potash, and about two and a half pints of water. Boil the whole together for some time, stirring the ingredients occasionally. The liquor may then be allowed to cool.

With a pointed stick, or dibble, make holes wherever the soil is infested. Drop the mixture, filling the holes full once or twice.

Fill small vials two-thirds with water, and add sweet-oil to float on the water to within half an inch of the top. Plunge these upright in the ground, leaving only half an inch standing out, near the nest or runs of the ants. The ants will come for a sip and go home to die. No insect can exist with oil stopping up its spiracles, or breathing pores.

Boiling water and arsenic are fatal; coarse sponge dipped in treacle-water, and afterwards dipped in scalding water, will catch thousands.

May be destroyed by a few fresh, unpicked bones being placed for them, or sponges wetted and filled with sugar, or treacle in bottles or pans.

VARIOUS INSECTS.

Wiggle-tails.

Wiggle-tails sometimes get into a tub of plants. A small fish, say perch, caught in any stream or pond will keep the water entirely free from this pest, and mosquitoes will not bother.

Keep the tub full as it evaporates. Just fill up with fresh water; no need to bail the water. A lady kept a perch in a tub of water-lilies, and the tub was free from all pests of the kind.

Gooseberry Saw-fly.

Dust white hellebore over the leaves in same manner as Paris green is dusted over the patch. It is sure destruction. If mixed with water there will be no danger from the inhalation of the powder. An ounce to a pailful of water is a good proportion.

Rose-chafer.

Spread sheets under plants attacked. Shake well; the insects will fall and may be quickly destroyed.

Radish-fly.

Hot water has been used with some success.

Cockroaches, Crickets, etc.

Place bell-glasses, bottles, smooth or glazed pans, so that the sides are in a slanting position, and fill them with treacle and water, in which the insects drown themselves.

Cockroaches may be destroyed with certainty by using a mixture of one part arsenic, one part white sugar, and one part lard, all the three to be white. It is essential that the arsenic be white, or failure will result.

Destruction of Cockchafers.

A French gardener adopted this ingenious method: "After sunset I place in the centre of my orchard an old barrel, the inside of which I have previously well tarred. At the bottom of the barrel I place a lighted lamp. Insects of many kinds, attracted by the light, make for the lamp, and while circling round it strike against the sides of the barrel, where, meeting with the tar, their wings and legs become so clogged that they fall helpless to the bottom. In the morning I examine the barrel, and frequently take out of it ten or twelve gallons of cockchafers, which I at once destroy. A few cet*t*' worth of tar employed in this way will, without any further trouble, be the means of destroying innumerable numbers of these insects, whose larvæ are amongst the most destructive pests the gardener or farmer has to contend against."

To Destroy Black Beetles.

A certain remedy is to procure some bracken, *Pteris aquilina*, or common fern, plentiful on commons, and put it down about the house at night. The black beetle will eat it ravenously and soon die. It is commonly used in the north of England.

Insect Enemies of the Cabbage.

A *small black flea* in great swarms eats the leaves of cabbage-plants, after being set out in the open ground from hot-beds. A slight dusting of fresh-slacked lime over the plants in the morning, while wet with dew, will drive them off or kill them. Dust the plants one morning, and again the second morning after that; then the job is finished. The flea is more fond of pepper-cress than cabbages, so that if the cress is sown thinly along with the cabbage-seed it will save the cabbages.

Lice on Cabbages.—A greenish, mealy louse, in vast numbers, attacks cabbages when nearly full grown. Two dustings of fresh lime will kill them.

Grubs.—A black grub, which lodges in the ground, eats through the stems of young cabbages after being transplanted, causing the heads to drop off. Whenever that is observed, search around the plants cut off, and find the grub and kill it. It is only a quarter of an inch under the surface. After it eats off one plant it gets to another; so that you must search among the neighboring plants, if not found where it has been devastating.

Cabbage-lice.—As soon as the plant begins to head, or as the louse makes its appearance, open the leaves carefully with the fingers, and sprinkle common salt between them. This has been used with such success that many gardeners consider it infallible. Plants used in this way produce larger and more solid heads than those left to themselves.

A California gardener used two tablespoonfuls of kerosene mixed with a pint of water, and applied by rubbing it on the outside leaves. A couple of applications is usually sufficient.

Cabbage-fly on Flowers.—The cabbage-fly sometimes infests the *sweet alyssum* and other sweet-scented flowers.

A syringing with water in which a few drops of coal-oil has been spread will soon dispose of him.

Cabbage Cut-worms.—Put fresh-cut grass, cornstalks, etc., in heaps here and there in the cabbage-patch. During the night the larvæ will find and crawl within, and are easily captured and destroyed.

Another method will be to wind sized paper closely around the plants, banking it slightly with a little loose earth. Nothing can climb up this smooth surface.

MILDEW.

Mildew on Roses.

Carbolic soap, well diluted in water, will destroy mildew on roses. It is to be applied by sprinkling.

A good wash to prevent mildew is with a sponge and soft-soap water, made with three or four ounces of soft-soap to a gallon of water; the soap should be dissolved in cold water.

VARIOUS WASHES FOR TREES AND SHRUBS.

Throw slacked lime as a dust over trees and bushes when the foliage is wet.

Syringe with soap-suds, or tobacco-water, or a strong decoction of quassia with soap-suds. Chloride of lime, a weak solution, will preserve plants from insects; sprinkle well over them.

Red Spider on Currant and Gooseberry Bushes.

A gardener has used soluble sulphur in large quantities for the destruction of red spider on gooseberry and currant bushes, and prepares it as follows: "I slack some quicklime, and mix it with about half its weight of common flour of sulphur in a heap, with a little water, as in making mortar. After lying a few hours I boil it for twenty minutes in a large boiler of water in about the proportion of one gallon to one pound of the mixture. This produces a sulphurous liquid, about the color of porter, two or three pints of which to a two-gallon bucket of water is strong enough for syringing; but we test the strength by dipping a spray into the bucket, and get the liquor just strong enough not to damage the leaf; if too strong the leaf withers in an hour or two."

Washes for Fruit-trees

Lime and Sulphur.—Take of quick or unslacked lime four parts, and of common flour of sulphur one part; break up the lime in small pieces, then mix the sulphur with it in an iron vessel; pour on them enough boiling water to slack the lime to a powder; cover the vessel close as soon as the water is poured on. This makes a most excellent whitewash for orchard trees, and is very useful as a preventive of blight on pear-trees, to cover the wounds in the form of a paste when cutting away diseased parts, also for coating the trees in early spring.

It may be considered as a specific for many noxious insects and mildew in the orchard and nursery. Its material should always be ready at hand; it should be used quite fresh, since it soon loses its potency. This preparation should be sprinkled over the young plant as soon or before any trouble from aphides, thrips, or mildew occurs, early in the morning while the dew is on the trees. This lime and sulphur combination is destructive to these nests in this way, giving off gaseous sulphurous compounds, which are deadly poison to minute life, both animal and fungoid; while the lime destroys by contact the same things, and its presence is noxious to them. In moderate quantities it is not injurious to common vegetable life.

Another recipe for a wash for orchard trees is to put one-half bushel of lime and four pounds of powdered sulphur into a tight barrel, slacking the lime with hot water, the mouth of the barrel being covered with a cloth; this is reduced to the consistency of ordinary whitewash, and one-half ounce of carbolic acid is added to each gallon of liquid at the time of application. Apply to the trunk; it will not hurt the branches or foliage if applied to them also.

An experienced fruit-grower recommends the use of the following simple method: He takes lye from wood-ashes or common potash, mixes a little grease with it, heats quite warm, and with a little syringe throws it up into all parts of the tree, branches and trunk. It will effectually kill all kinds of caterpillars and worms that are infesting the tree or running over the bark. Trees treated in this manner are exceedingly healthy and vigorous in appearance, possessing a smooth, glossy bark.

An Excellent Wash for Garden Trees for the destruction of Moss.—Take sal-soda, which costs at retail from three to six cents per pound; place it in a skillet on the fire; it will soon go to what seems water, then evaporate and leave a white powder; keep it on the fire till it becomes a light brown, when it is done. Use a fourth of a pound, or, if the trees are much covered with moss or are very dirty, use half a pound to the gallon of water. Wash the trunks and large limbs, using a sponge or cloth. It can be used at any season of the year, but winter is preferable. This wash will not injure the foliage of the most delicate plant. In a few weeks after using, the trees will look as clean and sleek as though they had been varnished, and their growth and healthy appearance will be most astonishing. This is probably the best and cheapest wash for this purpose for garden use that can be suggested.

Experiments with Carbolic Soap.

An Ohio horticulturist succeeded in various experiments with carbolic soap as follows:

Cut-worms.—" For cut-worms I made the soap-suds pretty strong—two gallons of water to half a pound of soap—and with it saturated a bushel of sawdust, then placed a little around the stem of each cabbage and tomato plant, using a handful to eight or ten plants, adding a little more after two or three days when the odor seemed gone. This was completely successful in ground where the worms were quite plenty, and where plants not protected were speedily cut off by them. It is the cheapest and most easily applied remedy for garden insects that I have yet seen."

Striped Bugs.—"For striped bugs on melons and cucumber-vines I find the same method of using the soap quite effective, if the sawdust is sprinkled on the plants every day, which is very little trouble; but the plants may be wet directly with weak suds, made of ten gallons of water to half a pound of soap."

Aphis Plant-lice.—"For aphis or plant-lice on cherry-trees and the like a sprinkling or two with the suds by means of a sponge, or bending the shoots so as to dip them into a pail or basin, is speedy death to the bugs. Care must be used not to have the suds too strong when applied to tender plants or young shoots of trees."

Grape-vine Worms.—Carbolic-acid washes are certain death to worms that infest the leaves of grape-vines. A pound of the article dissolved in fifteen or twenty gallons of water will form a large quantity, which can be forced by a syringe over the entire vine, one or two applications drive away everything of insect nature.

Wash for Peach-trees, etc.—For all garden fruit-trees use it in the proportion of one pound of soap to ten gallons of water; sprinkle well over the bark, and ants, worms, borers, flies will all flee.

Experiments on Garden Trees, Shrubs, etc., with Carbolic Soap.—The editor of the *Horticulturist*, after various experiments, says: "We found that for the large measure-worm, which so often infests our city trees and grape-vines, a decoction of the Carbolic Plant Protector, sufficiently strong to kill or dislodge the worm itself, was strong enough to scorch and injure the leaves of the vines also. But for bark-lice and more tender worms and insects it was a most beneficial agent. It is especially useful and preventive against future attacks of insects. If plants are syringed freely once or twice a week the odor alone will repel insects, while there is no doubt the eggs of future progeny are destroyed also. Our first application to the grape-vines destroyed the worms, but scorched the leaves and retarded the ripening of the fruit. This was the effect, probably, of being too strong. The odor, however, remained in the garden and on the ground for several weeks, and there was no attack of insects thereafter. Some caterpillar-nests were also discovered, but a thorough soaking soon placed them all out of danger.

"For clearing the barks of any trees infested with lice or scales, or to keep off worms or borers, it is most excellent. We have seen worms writhe in agony when under the fumes of the acid, and a single touch of the raw substance upon their backs has killed them in thirty seconds, the effects upon the skin being like that of red-hot iron scorching."

This experience has been confirmed by a Pennsylvania gardener, who says:

"I have tried it upon various species of plants, and it has proved as efficacious in destroying insects and preventing their ravages upon plants as whale-oil soap, when properly applied. When syringed upon the plants, a pound to twelve or fourteen gallons of soft water has proved effective and safe; but to wash the stems of trees, make it doubly strong—say, to trees two inches in diameter, one pound Protector to six gallons of water; and tree-stems eight inches in diameter, four or five gallons of water to one pound of potatoes, and so on. It is an excellent thing to syringe plum-trees before they expand their bloom and after their fruit is set.

"It will also prove a capital safeguard against the various species of tree-borers and the peach cut-worm; but it must be used with caution, as it is very strong. Cultivators should weaken it well for first trial, and increase its strength gradually until they see its beneficial effects upon different species of plants.

"Rabbits in winter will hardly attack trees strongly coated with the Protector if they can get any other food."

Phosphorus Soap.

A cultivator who had not been successful with any of the common remedies in destroying insects at last found phosphorus soap super-excellent for both house, green-house, and garden.

A tablespoonful dissolved in a gallon of water, ap

HOW TO DESTROY INSECTS. 89

plied with a watering-pot or syringe, will completely clear the plants of insects. It is also a valuable fertilizer for all kinds of flowers.

To Destroy Moss and Insects on Fruit-trees.

One year some fruit-trees in the grounds of an amateur horticulturist in France were covered with moss and insects. The next season the same trees could hardly be recognized, their barks being smooth, glossy, and healthy. The recipe is as follows:

"Boil two gallons of barley in water, and then take out the barley, which can be given to the fowls. In this water dissolve three gallons of quick-lime. When it is cold mix two pounds of lamp-black, stirring it for a long time with a stick; then a pound and a half of flowers of sulphur (brimstone) and a quart of alcohol. Daub the trees with this by means of a paint-brush, after having scraped off the moss with a rough brush. This composition destroys the coccus, the grub, moss, and insects, gives strength and suppleness to the bark, and certainly revives the aspect of fruit-trees."

Gas-tar Water for Garden Insects.

Insects, worms, etc., on melons, cucumbers, cabbages, etc., may be destroyed by gas-tar water as follows:

"Get a barrel with a few gallons of gas-tar in it, pour water on the tar, always have it ready when needed, and when the bugs appear give them a liberal drink of the tar-water from a garden-sprinkler; if the rain washes it off and they return, repeat the dose."

It has also in some cases disposed of the Colorado potato-beetle.

Plant Remedies for Insects.

The seeds of the absinthium maritimum are deadly to the flea.

The odor of the alder is very obnoxious to most insects.

On a hot summer day cattle may be seen clustering around the alder bushes, wherever in their fields, for protection against the stings of flies.

The perfume of the chamomile is destructive of the acarus scabiei, and it is used in many pomades for the treatment of scabies.

An infusion of chamomile flowers has been recommended as a wash to the skin, for the purpose of protection against gnats, who shun the traitorous perfume.

To Prepare Lime-dust.

Take a peck of fresh or sharp lime, broken up into small pieces, then add four pounds of flowers of sulphur, or in like proportions if in smaller quantity.

Add one-third as much boiling water, or just enough to slack the lime to dry powder, and cover the vessel as soon as the water is poured on. By adding water it

HOW TO DESTROY INSECTS.

may be made into an excellent whitewash for trees, the sulphur increasing its efficacy.

Ground Aphis on Verbenas.

The ground aphis sometimes preys upon the roots of verbenas, causing the plant to appear as if mildewed. These insects are destroyed by washing the soil with a tepid decoction of tobacco, about the color of strong green tea, every day for a week or ten days.

Moles in Flower-beds.

a. Catch in traps.

b. Destroy by placing pieces of raw meat rubbed with stick phosphorus in their runs.

c. Plant the ricinus, or castor-oil bean, in the ground where they make their runs. This is called the mole-plant, because of this peculiar property. Those who have tried this remedy have found it unvarying in its success.

Traps.

Get some cabbage-leaves, warm them in an oven till hog's lard will spread on the surface; place them over night near your favorite plants, and almost every slug will be found under them in the morning. There must be no salt in the lard.

PART III.

INSECTS IN THE HOUSE.

ANTS.

Red Ants.

a. A SMALL bag of *sulphur* kept in a drawer or cupboard will drive away red ants.

b. Scatter branches of *sweet fern* where they congregate.

c. Place half-picked bones of meat here and there on the shelves and wherever the ants resort, and on visiting them an hour afterward they will be covered with ants. Have a bucket of scalding water in hand, and drop the swarming bones into it. Many thousands may be destroyed by this plan.

d. Pieces of coarse sponge dipped in treacle (molasses) water will do as well as the bones.

e. Sugar-boxes and barrels and anything in the house can be freed from ants by drawing a wide chalk mark just around the edge of the top of them. The mark

HOW TO DESTROY INSECTS. 93

must be unbroken, or they will creep over it, but a continuous chalk-mark half an inch in width will set their depredations at naught.

f. A house that was infested with ants by the myriads was thoroughly cleansed as follows:

Baits of raw meat were laid, which were speedily covered with them. These were rinsed in hot water and relaid.

Two men were thus engaged for two days actively at work, and no apparent diminution. All the woodwork of kitchen, cellar, and scullery was examined. All the woodwork and walls were covered with a good dose of fresh hot lime-whiting, and afterward these places were fumigated with sulphur for three or four days.

All the nooks, corners, chimneys, fireplaces, mantels were examined, and every crevice, haunt, etc., dosed with quicklime. Then the pest ceased, and never gave trouble again.

g. Take naphtha and scatter on them or around where they gather.

BEDBUGS.

a. Powdered alum or borax will keep bedbugs or chintz-bugs away, and travellers will find it very advantageous to carry a bundle of it in their hand-bags to scatter under or over their pillows or beds in hotels. A gentleman who used it says: "While staying at a hotel once with a party, most of whom complained sadly **of the nightly attacks of these** disgusting insects, I was able to keep them entirely at bay by its use, and I distributed the contents of my bundle among the party, **to their great relief."**

b. Scald **with hot water every crack** where they find refuge. Be careful **not to let the** water touch the varnish. **If it should by accident, it may be** restored by **rubbing immediately with a rag wet in** turpentine **or oil.**

c. **Fill crevices with salt, and** wash bedstead **with brine, or use kerosene in same** way.

d. **Paris green and** mercurial ointments are deadly **poisons to the bugs, but are** dangerous **to use in the house.**

e. **One part quicksilver to** twenty parts white **of an egg,** applied **with a feather to** every **crack and crevice in a** bed-room, **will kill them.**

f. Mix together one **ounce of corrosive** sublimate, **one** of gum camphor, one **pint of spirits of turpentine, and one of** alcohol. **Put the mixture in a bottle and apply** with a feather**; but be very careful, for it is rank poison.** They can also be destroyed by an ointment composed of quicksilver **and** benzine.

The proportions of the mixture may **be varied as follows:** one quarter pound of corrosive sublimate, one ounce **of camphor gum,** one half gallon of benzine, one half gallon **of hot water;** paint with a brush every crack and crevice, bedstead, etc.

g. Dust well the bedstead, crevices, and niches where they are with cayenne pepper.

COCKROACHES.

a. Gum camphor is one of the best things ever found; they always take quick leave where that is introduced. Scatter it upon the shelves, and in the corners of the pantry, and through closets, and these vermin will leave. The only trouble is that it evaporates so soon that it needs renewal every week. Spirits of camphor, although more evanescent than the gum, will hasten their departure more speedily.

b. Powdered borax, sprinkled around infested places, drives them away at once.

c. Sweetened vinegar and strychnine will destroy any house-bug.

d. The small land terrapin, commonly called "conter," wages unrelenting war against them if placed where they frequent. He is more successful than any of the powders.

e. "The best thing I have ever tried is a quantity of red wafers, such as were used to seal letters in old times, thrown where the roaches mostly hide, under the floors or in the bottom of presses—in fact, anywhere they can be safely put out of reach of children. R."

f. "I give a recipe to your correspondent who wishes to know how to get rid of the insects he calls cockroaches, although I think he misnames them. Let his wife finish making peach preserves late at night in a smooth, bright brass kettle; then persuade her it is too late to clean the kettle till morning, but set it against the wall where the insects are thickest, and retire to rest. In the morning he will find the sides of the kettle bright as a new dollar, but he will find every insect that was hungry in the bottom of the kettle, when, if he uses the recipe as I did, he will treat them to a sufficient quantity of boiling water to render them perfectly harmless. As I thought molasses cheaper than peach-preserve juice, I ever afterwards baited the same trap with molasses, and I caught the last one of millions. I pity any person troubled with them. I have lived thirty years since making the discovery (accidental), and have never had to repeat it. UNCLE JOHN."

g. Sprinkle the floor with hellebore at night; they will eat it and be poisoned.

MOTHS.

No. 1. Make a solution of one ounce of gum camphor, one ounce of powdered red pepper, in eight ounces of alcohol; let stand for one week, and strain. Sprinkle the furs or cloth with it, and wrap in cloth or strong paper.

To keep them out of carpets wash floor with turpentine or benzine before laying them.

No. 2. Dust furs with powdered alum, working it in well at the roots of the hair. Do not air woollen articles and furs in the summer sunshine. They should be put aside in the early spring, and left untouched until October.

Moths in Carpets, Woollens, etc.

a. Several pieces of camphor gum, as large as hickory-nuts, should be packed in with all woollen garments and furs. Infested garments or furs should be put in a tight sack or trunk, and, after adding a half-ounce of chloroform, the sack or trunk should be closed as nearly air-tight as possible. The vapor will kill the insects.

b. For furniture and carpets, heavy paper, wet with carbolic acid or spirits of turpentine, will kill larvæ already at work. This should be placed under the edge of the carpet where the mischief is generally done, and in furniture crowded back in the deep folds. Russian leather, cedar bark or boughs, tobacco-leaves, and even red pepper, are said to prevent the moths from laying eggs.

c. Another way of destroying moths in carpets is to take a wet sheet or other cloth, lay it upon the carpet, and then run a hot flat-iron over it, so as to convert the water into steam, which permeates the carpet beneath and destroys the moth and her eggs. It can be done without taking up the carpet, and has proved, after trials, remarkably efficient.

d. To prevent moths, use camphor, Persian powder, or benzine freely. Wrap clean woollens carefully in paper or cotton cloths, and they will be secure unless they are soiled; moths will attack soiled places. If moths are already in your carpets, wring a coarse cloth out of clean water, spread it smoothly on the part of the carpet where the moths are, or are suspected to be, and iron it with a pretty hot iron. The steam will destroy both the moths and eggs. Also, take boiling-hot alum-water and dip cloths into it, and saturate the carpets with it. Moths deposit their eggs in the early part of the spring, and that is the time to attend to furs. Beat the furs with a light rattan, and air them for several hours; then carefully comb them with a clean coarse comb, wrap them up in newspapers perfectly tight, and put them away in a tight linen bag or a chest. Examine them several times during the summer, and repeat the combing process.

Woollen articles can be kept from moths by dusting them over with red pepper or putting camphor gum among them.

FLEAS.

Coal-oil will kill fleas either on animals or in the house. The addition of a small quantity of oil pennyroyal improves it. Another effectual exterminator which can be used on house dogs and cats without causing any inconvenience is the **Persian** insect powder (flowers of the *Pyrethrum carneum*), growing upon the Caucasian mountains, and imported into this country and used extensively for the above purpose, and sold by druggists in the form of Lyon's, Drake's, and other insect powders, in small bottles, retailing for twenty-five cents. Any druggist can order it in bulk, costing from 75 cents to $1 per pound. Better to get the whole flowers and powder them yourself, as it is often adulterated with chamomile and other worthless flowers. This is very sure death to fleas, and the writer has collected a tablespoonful of fleas from a small dog in a few minutes after use. Sprinkle the powder over the animal and see that it comes in contact with the vermin. It is perfectly harmless, and also said to be certain death to bedbugs and roaches.

Sprinkle about a few drops of oil of lavender.

FLIES.

Paint walls or rub over picture-frames with laurel-oil.

CONTENTS.

	PAGE		PAGE
Alum-water	32	Cockchafers	79
Ants	76	Cockroaches, etc.	79
Ants in the House	92	"	95
Ants, Black, on Peonies	19	Codling Moth	75
Ants, Potash for	50	Cold Water	46
Aphis	8, 9, 12, 86, 91	Colorado Potato-beetle	74
Aster-bugs	73	Cucumber-beetle	75
Bark-louse	70	" bug	74
Bed-bugs	93	Currant-louse	69
Black Beetles	80	" worms	67
Borer and Bark-louse	70	" "	66
Cabbage-lice	81	Earth-worms	20
Cabbage-fly	81	Epsom Salts	56
" Cut-worms	81	Fertilizers for House Plants	54
" Insect Enemies	80	Fleas	98
" Worms	63, 64, 65	Flies	25
Canker-worm Remedy	68	"	99
Canker-worms	68	Frost-bitten Plants	87
Carbolic Soap-suds	5	Fumigating	14, 15, 16
" "	12	Gas-tar Water	89
" Soap	85	Good Wash for Plants	55
Caterpillars	60	Gooseberry-grubs	71
" on Cabbage, etc.	60	Gooseberry Saw Fly	78
" on Gooseberries	61	Grape-vine Worms	86
Coal-oil	31	Green Bugs	45, 46
"	56	" Fly	8, 12, 28

CONTENTS.

	PAGE
Green Lice	24
Grubs in Flower-gardens	71
" in Pots	23
Hellebore for Caterpillars	62
House Insects	32
Insects on Rose-bushes	53
Kerosene	31
Leaf-lice on Fruit-trees	69
Lice on Rose-bushes	51
Lime-dust	90
Lime-water for Worms	20
Manure-water	37
May-bugs	73
Mealy-bug	17
" "	39
" "	48
" " on Grape-vines	72
Mildew on Roses	82
" "	29
Moles in Flower-beds	91
Moles, Traps	91
Moss and Insects	89
Moths	96
"	97
Oleander-bugs	24
Onion-maggot	69
Paris Green	29
Pear-slugs	57
Persian Insect Powder	12
Phosphorus Soap	88
Plant-lice	24
Plant Parasites	36
Plant Remedies	90
Plaster-of-Paris	56
Plum-slugs	59
Quassia for Rose-bugs	52

	PAGE
Quassia-tea	10
Radish-fly	79
Raspberry-worms	67
Red Pepper	50
Red Spider, Remedies. 5, 6, 7, 28, 82	
Rose-bugs	27
Rose-chafer	79
Rose-grubs	30
" "	71
" Insect Enemies	26
" slugs	52
" "	31, 30
Salt and Hot Water	44
Salt for Roses	54
Scale	18
" Louse	39
" on Ivy	25
Scotch Snuff	30
Slugs on Begonias	19
" on Cabbages	58
" on Cherries	58
" on Jessamines	60
" on Currants	58
" Rose	26
Snails	25
Soot-tea	37
Squash-bugs	72
Stimulants	51
Striped Bug	74
" Bugs	86
Submerging Plants	16
Sulphur	51
Thrips	7
"	43
Tobacco-powder	9
" in Dish	15

CONTENTS.

	PAGE		PAGE
Tobacco-tea	34	White Spots on Window-sills.	36
" for Green Bugs	45	" Worms	20
" water	32	Wiggletails	78
Tomato-worms	68	Wire-worms	65
Verbenas, Aphis	91	Wood-lice	70, 71
Verbena-rust	41	" "	19
Wash for Garden-trees	84	Worms on Honeysuckle Vines	67
Washes for Fruit-trees	83	" on Lawns	67
Whale-oil Soap	34	" in Pots	20, 21, 22. 23
White Hellebore	19	Yellows	29

www.ingramcontent.com/pod-product-compliance
Lightning Source LLC
Chambersburg PA
CBHW020156170426
43199CB00010B/1068